A   3 <u>95</u>

MEDITATIONS ON HOPE AND LOVE

D1649173

Meditations
on Hope and Love

KARL RAHNER

A Crossroad Book
THE SEABURY PRESS • NEW YORK

1977
The Seabury Press
815 Second Avenue
New York, N.Y. 10017

Published originally under the titles *Was sollen wir jetz tun?* and *Gott ist Mensch geworden*
© 1974, 1975 by Verlag Herder KG Freiburg im Breisgau

This translation and arrangement © 1976 by Search Press Limited

The translation was made by V. Green

Library of Congress Cataloging in Publication Data

Rahner, Karl, 1904-
Meditations on hope and love.

Translation of Was sollen wir jetz tun? and Gott ist Mensch geworden.
"A Crossroad book."
1. Christmas—Meditations. I. Rahner, Karl, 1904-
Gott ist Mensch geworden. English. 1977.   II. Title.
BV45.R2513   1977   242'.33   77-76614
ISBN 0-8164-2155-2

Printed in the United States of America

Contents

PART ONE

1 The last days and the Lord's coming

Jesus told the apostles: And there will be signs in sun and moon and stars, and upon the earth distress of nations in perplexity at the roaring of the sea and the waves, men fainting with fear and with foreboding of what is coming on the world; for the powers of the heavens will be shaken. And then they will see the Son of man coming in a cloud with power and great glory. Now when these things begin to take place, look up and raise your heads, because your redemption is drawing near . . . But take heed to yourselves lest your hearts be weighed down with dissipation and drunkenness and cares of this life, and that day come upon you suddenly like a snare; for it will come upon all who dwell upon the face of the whole earth. But watch at all times, praying that you may have strength to escape all these things that will take place, and to stand before the Son of man (Luke 21. 25-8. 34-6).

You will probably have noticed that in its liturgy the Church uses disturbing texts which are difficult to explain and whose meaning isn't clear to us at first sight. That seems to be the case with this Advent reading. Of course we can easily divide it into three parts: the signs of the end of the world; the coming of the Son of man, which arouses courage and hope; and a warning to beware of the cares of everyday life.

Advent really means future. The inward readiness required in Advent is contemplation of the start of God's coming into our world (the 'first' coming of the word of God made flesh into our world). It is also contemplation of the fulfilment of that very same coming (the 'second' coming of the Son of man).

I

1.   In the first two verses of the text Jesus speaks of the signs that announce the end of the world and its history. He uses words that we don't understand when we hear them the first time. That doesn't mean that we can't today conceive of an end to the world. That kind of end of human history as such is a more rational prediction for us than for past generations. But a question remains: What has such a utopian or rationally conceivable end of the world to do with us here and now and with our religious life?

It is very hard to accept that when the end of humankind does come, the sun will really grow dark, the moon cease to give light, the stars fall from the sky, and 'the powers in the heaven' be shaken, as the parallel text in Mark 13. 25 puts it. But we do have to understand these prophecies of a cosmic catastrophe as referring to the end of human history. They ask to be interpreted quite radically if any sense at all is to be got out of them. But what are we to make of the first two verses of the text?

First we have to realize that Jesus is not a reporter back from a mission to a future end of the world which he has to all intents and purposes already experienced, and is trying to describe as it really is (which means in a way that Jesus' human mind, like ours, can't be aware of). Jesus isn't looking back to us from that future. Instead he is with us. He is looking together with us, forward to an inconceivable future. In the ultimate depths of his existence before God he knows of the end of everything and accepts that the reality of the world and of history will come to an end.

That inward knowledge of the transience of all things takes on a kind of outward, objective pictorial life. It emerges in terms of the images available to Jesus in the mental and linguistic world of his time.

What Jesus wants to describe is the tendency to end which is inherent in all human and earthly reality. He is citing the way in which all reality has a religiously absolute significance which is accepted by a man of faith who wants to live in accordance with the will of God. Because he looks forward to the end of the world (and not back from it), because he looks from the innermost experience of finiteness and the death-destined nature of his own human existence as a life approved by God, Jesus sees his own death and the collapse of the religious and political society to which he belongs. He sees the end of the world in the very same perspective, although that does not mean that he is interested in knowing how long the intervals of time between those events are. Therefore he speaks out of a profound experience of that finiteness which is also our own, if only we do not suppress it but are ready to accept it.

All that Jesus has to say of the outward events leading up to the end of the world recalls our actual internal and external memories of disappointments, illness, pain, growing old, failures and people dying; experiences we live through and suppress; experiences which always have an inward and an outward aspect; experiences which are our own and those of the world at the same time.

11

We celebrate Advent by perceiving and accepting those indications of the end of the world in our life. We should accept them realistically, and in a hope which is final and supreme and authenticated in itself and not from without.

Our hope is then that that absolute end will be a blessed resolution of all things. Signs of such a culmination meet a Christian everywhere in his life. When he dies, that end which is completion has arrived for him.

2.   That end, which is both individual and the end of the world, is, so the second part of the text says, identical with the coming of the Son of man. Here we presuppose that Jesus identifies himself with that Son of man; that the coming in a cloud accords with an image used in Daniel 7. 13 (an expression for the status which God gives the Son of man). We acknowledge what is said in the text when we say the Apostles' Creed and pray: Thence he will come to judge both the living and the dead. Of course we have no reason to think of this coming of the Lord as something local, as a process we can see with our eyes. If we look at it more closely, we can see how wrong that would be.

The process which by the grace of God moves the world and its history towards fulfilment, and which entered into a triumphant and irreversible phase in the death and Resurrection of Jesus, is the coming of Christ. At least, it will be the coming of Christ when that process reaches its end: its completion or fulfilment. Everyone then will be with Christ. When Christian hope summons us to await the coming of Christ, that means that we take our place in faith, hope and love in the process propelling the world towards everlasting fulfilment of the universe and of history in God by virtue of its participation in Jesus' death and Resurrection. That means that as free Christian men and women we are liberated from all powers and all compulsion in our existence and that no thing or event can have the last word in our lives. We expect and await that last word of forgiveness, grace, freedom and fulfilment from that which we know as God, who has already promised it to us in Jesus and in his life and death. It means too that he will grant us that last word (which — ultimately — he himself is), when in death and in the end all our own answers are transformed into a question: a single question that we ourselves are no longer able to answer. If this word of God's is spoken, and the end which is fulfilment comes about, then the Son of man will have come, for the word of God begins in him, and begins there definitively and triumphantly.

3.   The theme of the third section of the present text occurs more emphatically in the text for the third meditation.

II

Now let us look at Advent as a whole. In the winter season in which European Christians generally celebrate Advent, the world grows quieter. Everything round-about becomes flat and colourless. It seems as if the world has grown subdued, chastened; as if it has lost its courage or self-assertion and its readiness to declare that it is proud of its power and life. In this part of the year, time shows the world its poverty; the world offers us a certain disillusionment. Everything becomes fleeting. The world continually loses into the past what it appears to gain from the future and to take into its own present.

    Then it is up to time to overcome the sadness of the times. It has to tell itself quietly and firmly what faith tells us. It is a time in which to speak the word of faith in the spirit of faith: I believe in the eternity of God which has entered into our time and therefore into my time. Secretly, beneath the swell of time, life already grows, life that no longer knows death. It is there already; in me already. It is in me because I have faith. How little I have to do for the wheel of birth and death to stand still in reality. All I must do is to believe in God's advent in our time; to believe by patiently enduring time, its harsh and unrelenting robbery and its allowing things and people to die; to believe that this time does not have the last word, that No in the end is not everything.

God has already begun to celebrate his advent in the world and in me. Softly and gently, so softly that it is possible to miss him, he has already taken the world and its world-time to his heart. He has put his own inconceivable life into this time of ours. We call that victory over fear of fleeting time, the grace of faith. And faith recognizes that God made this dying time in order to redeem it by taking it into his own eternity. There is an eternal now in us that has no nothingness any more: neither a nothingness past nor a nothingness to come. That *now* has already begun to collect our earthly moments and to take them into itself.

We do not rejoice with loud rejoicing in this Advent season. It lasts a lifetime, after all, and it makes such insistent demands on our poor hearts. There is no great rejoicing for we still feel, all too surely, the burdensome chains of time upon us. But within ourselves we ought to feel something living: the calm and modest joy of faithful hope which does not think that the graspable visible present is all that there is. That quiet joy is what a prisoner feels when he is still in his cell but is about to stand up, for he knows that the lock hangs loose at his cell door and that his freedom is certain. Is this joy, our Advent joy, so very hard to bear?

2 Making ready the way

In the fifteenth year of the reign of Tiberius Caesar, Pontius Pilate being governor of Judea, and Herod being tetrarch of Galilee, and his brother Philip tetrarch of the region of Ituraea and Trachonitis, and Lysanias tetrarch of Abilene, in the high-priesthood of Annas and Caiaphas, the word of God came to John the son of Zecharaiah in the wilderness; and he went into all the region about the Jordan, preaching a baptism of repentance for the forgiveness of sins. As it is written in the book of the words of Isaiah the prophet, 'The voice of one crying in the wilderness: Prepare the way of the Lord, make his paths straight. Every valley shall be filled, and every mountain and hill shall be brought low, and the crooked shall be made straight, and the rough ways shall be made smooth; and all flesh shall see the salvation of God' (Luke 3. 1-6).

With this text Luke begins his version of the public life of Jesus. In the first two chapters, of course, he has told the story of Jesus' infancy. Because Luke so to speak begins all over again with this third chapter of his gospel, and since he is now recounting the events which make Jesus' infancy (as Luke sees it) significant and credible for us, the 'second beginning' has a chronological reference to the year 28-9 of our era, to the time of the Emperor Tiberius, Augustus' stepson, in whose reign Jesus was born.

This formal opening and the reference to a specific time and political situation fit Luke's special theological intentions and ideas. New Testament theologians specializing in biblical salvation and redemption history think of Luke as the church theologian among the evangelists, for he sees the Church as entering into its own era (one, that is, with its own specific significance and importance) between the history of Jesus and the last days.

I should like to ask at this point a certain latitude in treating the text in a somewhat old-fashioned though no less relevant way.

The text speaks of John the Baptist as the forerunner of Jesus. Of course this function of the Baptist in regard to Jesus and his mission is a very special one; it isn't a function of our own lives. If however we try to discover a kind of 'forerunning' in our own lives, or to make it an important characteristic, then we have to remember the special problems and dangers of that kind of use of a particular biblical image. Nevertheless this kind of application of the Baptist story is justifiable in the sense that we receive strength to bear life's burdens when we learn that the history of salvation already features a situation which, in spite of its uniqueness, is rather like our own.

I am not concerned here with the substance of the Baptist's message, nor with the fact that a word is used of him and his activity that we already find in Isaiah 40 3-5. I am interested in the fact that Luke, like the other three evangelists, puts the figure of the Baptist at the beginning of the gospel of Jesus, and therefore portrays him from the start as a forerunner of Jesus.

That is not so obvious as it might at first seem.

About twenty-five years after the Baptist's death, so the Acts of the Apostles tell us (19. 1-7; 18. 25), in Ephesus, and therefore a long way away from Palestine, there were disciples of John who knew nothing of Jesus and his Church. The argument of the first chapter of John's gospel is directed against them too (1. 6-8; 15. 29-34). Therefore we can be sure that John the Baptist did not seem from the start to be no more than the Messiah's forerunner, the predecessor of one whom the Baptist from the start picked out and directly identified as Jesus. According to the gospels (Matthew 11. 2-6; Luke 7. 18-23), even at the end of his life (when he was in prison), the Baptist still wasn't wholly clear about Jesus' Messiahship. Therefore we are justified in seeing the clarity and lack of ambiguity with which the gospels present the relation between John the Baptist and Jesus, and quite straightforwardly and emphatically subordinate the Baptist to Jesus, partly as the result of theological reflection among the first Christians.

The first Christians had, in their understanding of Jesus, to come to terms with the astonishing fact that Jesus let himself be baptized as if he were a sinner. Therefore they could not ignore the relation between John and Jesus, as they did other religious movements and trends of the time, which are more or less uniformly passed over by the gospels. It is in that perspective that we have to see the special nature of John's activity.

John is indeed a forerunner. He precedes without sure and certain knowledge of whom or what he is serving. He may not himself share the immediate experience of the salvation that has become present in Jesus; he longingly foretells it. What he awaits and expects overtakes him without really catching up with him in the sense of his seeing clearly what he was aiming at.

His preaching of the coming of God as judgment is overtaken by Jesus' proclamation of the coming of God as liberation and forgiveness. John is the forerunner. He is that and no more, because he was that and did not wish to be anything more than that; because he was ready to humble himself; to diminish himself so that he who was to come could grow in stature; because he resigned himself to the task of the moment; for all those reasons he belongs to the history of Jesus and of ultimate salvation, and is blessed with the fulness of the future which he was able in his own time to greet longingly but only from afar.

Surely we are all forerunners? We are all pilgrims on the wearisome roads of our life. There is always something ahead of us that we have not yet overtaken. When we do catch up with something it immediately becomes an injunction to leave it behind us and to go onwards. Every end becomes a beginning. There is no resting place or abiding city. Every answer is a new question. Every good fortune is a new longing. Every victory is only the beginning of a defeat.

Surely we are forerunners? As parents we are the forerunners of our children. As old people, the forerunners of the young. As the scientists and scholars of today, the forerunners of those of tomorrow. As the politicians of today, the forerunners of those to come, who will scatter and suppress those of today.

We so quickly change the goals, words, and obvious characteristics of our projects, of politics, of the sciences, and of art. Every man seems to march into his present moment with the feeling that now the real thing is coming, the truly valid thing that is once and for all, only then — very soon, alas! — to perceive that his present is turning into past; that he is old-fashioned and out-of-date; that he no longer understands and is no longer understood.

Aren't we always despatching messengers from the

dungeon of our compulsions and disappointments? We send them to find the real thing, that which is ultimately valid, even though we do not really know where to direct these messengers of our unassuaged longing?

Isn't death, which swallows us all, the only thing that we are sure to catch up with on our way? In our strange confusion we try to hold back the fleeting moment and to get to the next moment ahead more quickly than ever it could get to us. We who on all human pathways are always forerunners of the transient are always tempted to elevate our plans and projects to the level of something that is to come, an ultimate that will remain for ever. It seems that something of the idiocy which makes a man see everything and everyone else as transitory and himself as ultimate, and refuse to be a mere forerunner of an incalculable future, is an almost inevitable feature of the world on its way.

Everywhere, always, we are no more than predecessors. The goal of our journeying seems always to remain far ahead of us, to stay beyond our power and always to fade into new perspectives of distance, even when we think we are approaching it.

We should remember the Advent spirit which John the Baptist, as Jesus' forerunner, experienced before us: a willing acceptance of the small, seemingly mundane task which this particular moment puts before us; a humble readiness to do the one small thing even when we see the greater thing that is denied us; unenvying preparedness to acknowledge a greater excellence in others, even when we cannot bask in the reflected glory; hope that the unutterable will come to us too in our restriction and imprisonment, from which we can no longer break out; the assurance that all finite things, even death, can be inwardly fulfilled by the eternal God of love and light, if only they are accepted in hope, and that every setback in life can be a resurgence; the certainty rising from all the graves of disappointments that even the cry in the wilderness will be heard by someone, and that all that sowing of our tears will bring forth a harvest of joy, even if only in the storehouses of eternal life; readiness to undertake a further journey even when we had thought that at last we were home for ever.

It is an Advent journey when we continue on our way and see coming towards us what we could never catch up with in our walking: God himself who secretly allowed us to go where we thought we were going — towards our own goals — and who gives us himself when tangible things are taken from us. After all, we ourselves are forerunners and everything tangible is transitory. He who innocently takes and innocently leaves as the moment asks, is in Advent; from him nothing will really be taken away, for everything that he has to leave behind him is only a sign that he has to go a longer way before he truly comes to the everlasting light — light and life eternal.

Life is a unique Advent. The question is: Are we ready to accept and celebrate it in that sense?

3 What shall we do?

And the multitudes asked him, 'What then shall we do?'
And he answered them, 'He who has two coats, let him
share with him who has none; and he who has food, let
him do likewise'. Tax collectors also came to be bap-
tized, and said to him, 'Teacher, what shall we do?'
And he said to them, 'Collect no more than is appointed
you.' Soldiers also asked him, 'And we, what shall we
do?' And he said to them, 'Rob no one by violence or
by false accusation, and be content with your wages.'
As the people were in expectation, and all men quest-
ioned in their hearts concerning John whether perhaps
he were the Christ, John answered them all, 'I baptize
you with water; but he who is mightier than I is coming,
the thong of whose sandals I am not worthy to untie;
he will baptize you with the Holy Spirit and with fire.
His winnowing fork is in his hand, to clear his threshing
floor, and to gather the wheat into his granary, but the
chaff he will burn with unquenchable fire.' So, with
many other exhortations, he preached good news to the
people (Luke 3. 10-18).

Luke tells us again of John the Baptist, the forerunner

of Jesus, and of his preaching.

The text is divided into two parts. In the first part, John answers his audience's question about the consequences for their lives of his basic message: the news of the imminent judgment and the demand that they should radically change their lives. In the second part, John rejects the claim that he is the Messiah, and that he can act as the mediator of the Spirit of the Kingdom that is to come.

The first section (with which I am mainly concerned here) is not so surprising. There is always the temptation to shrug off these moral injunctions as obvious, even as banal. But if we look at them closely, they are most compelling.

John is said to be the one whom Isaiah previously proclaimed as the voice in the wilderness, the one who was to announce God's coming salvation, the prophet of a final, imminent divine judgment, a last chance for radical conversion, the impossibility of satisfying God by anything other than a definitive conversion which fundamentally transforms all one's life from what it has been hitherto. And now people ask this preacher of a radical religious change and new start, what they actually have to do if they really want to obey that uncompromising message. The answer appears to be just a string of moralistic clichés, which you can find elsewhere, and which don't have to be preceded by any apocalyptic rant to make them comprehensible. Tax collectors mustn't make unjust demands; soldiers should be honourable men who don't terrorize the neighbourhood and are to be satisfied with their wages. John doesn't question, of course, the calling or work of the tax collectors and soldiers in the pay of the occupation authorities — work which for pious people then was very dubious and even contemptible.

Even when he goes on to say that they must share their food and clothing (if they have enough of them) with poor neighbours, John does not go beyond what seem to be the obvious dictates of common human morality. If we make a further list of advice in the same style for other professions and situations, the apparent contrast would remain between a radical command to change one's life and those everyday maxims which the Baptist's audience must certainly have been aware of, and followed or ignored, before they heard his sermon; and, good will apart, certainly didn't fulfil much more effectively once they had heard him in the vein of our text.

What does this mean? This gospel gives no direct answer. All we know is that these apparently contradictory things somehow go together and make sense.

We have all certainly had the experience that the demands of a seemingly ordinary, everyday morality are not so easy after all — as long, that is, as we do not fall into the error of counting as moral principles only what suits us and happens to be easy for us. Everyday life as it is already asks a lot of man as he is. To keep on through dull, tedious, everyday existence can often be more difficult than a unique deed whose heroism makes us run the danger of pride and self-satisfaction.

If we remember that the religious and moral value of life is more than the mere collective significance of individual moments; and that it forms a whole with its own character as that very whole, even when it is realized through the sum of individual actions; then a life spent in duties, in the constantly renewed will to be just and good to others, a life in which man does not allow himself to sink into tired resignation on account of the meaninglessness of his day, a life of good spirits which is a divine gift and virtue, and so forth; a life like that no longer stands in striking contrast to John's call to conversion. Such a life of apparently humdrum moral ordinariness in fact posits that conversion not as happening at a specific moment in time, but as a hidden principle permeating the apparently everyday nature of life as a whole.

But that is not all. What we make of the apparent contradiction does not depend on that. There is something else, imperceptible perhaps, here and there at least, in our performance of obvious everyday duties, some of which may even be of advantage to us.

In ordinary circumstances, life constantly manoeuvres us into situations in which the obvious aspect of humdrum chores disappears or seems absurd. Suddenly common morality just isn't worth it. Its banal meaning vanishes or has to change to something quite different. The meaningful utility of an action dies or moves into the realm of the holy. The duty remains unrewarded; indeed, doing it seems instead to be punished.

A respectable citizen is no longer the honourable man to whom people look up but a fool who just doesn't know how to get along in life. All of a sudden, people take incredible advantage of selflessness; they no longer respect honesty but even use it as a weapon against an honest man.

There are a thousand ways in which everyday morality can become a mysteriously awful thing, in all its obviousness and quite apart from any special heroic situations. It isn't worth it any longer; it no longer yields the measurable return which the doer himself got out of it. A reasonable and honourable egotism (which can also be a collective matter) becomes something quite different, or it's given up as unprofitable. It just doesn't pay — either in itself or us.

But what happens to that everyday virtuousness when it doesn't any longer pay, even in a sublime sort of way, and yet isn't given up as meaningless? It becomes a kind of 'forerunning' of the God of salvation and freedom. When we say that, the word 'God' must not be thought of as referring to anything else that we might connect with it. It means what it says. It means that what we mean by God is experienced precisely in this quiet but extraordinary transformation, just as it occurs in fulfilling our everyday morality.

God is the one whom we meet, even though perhaps without naming him, and unconsciously, when we dare to be foolish, when we avoid conflicts and power struggles that we had a chance of winning; when we love without the initial certainty of being loved in return; when we remain true to our convictions even to our disadvantage, and that disadvantage is not merely an episode in a battle we are sure to win in the end; when, to put it in a nutshell, we are true to our conscience and no longer confuse its demands with the claims of that obvious material utility and significance primarily (and quite justifiably) announced by everyday morality.

When such a demand of conscience transforms everyday morality behind its façade, if we refuse that challenge (perhaps quite unobtrusively) God is judging us. But it can be God coming as ultimate freedom, as saving freedom, if we obey the sudden call. That can happen quite quietly in the usual fulfilment of everyday duties. We seem to be moving along the well-worn paths of normal human conduct, rationally and respectably, behaving (even if with advantage to ourselves) with respect to others. Then, suddenly, in the twinkling of an eye, we are in the wilderness — God's saving wilderness.

If we recommend everyday morality and do not tacitly cancel the recommendation when it doesn't pay, we are in fact calling for a radical change of heart, even though we can't fix it at a specific point in time and life. Then we call on and praise the grace of God, which fills those depths to which the paths of our modest everyday life do in fact lead, right up to the point where we let ourselves fall fearlessly into that profundity.

What shall we do? Somewhat intimidated, people asked that question after John the Baptist's frightening sermon about sin and the inevitable judgment, about all-transforming conversion. John answered them; and suddenly his answer holds us just where we are, living quite ordinarily; where we are, carrying on patiently. His answer means that it is here precisely that we can experience the coming of the Kingdom of God, if only we want to, and if only we can surrender in hope to the hidden meaning and innermost power of this everyday life of ours.

4 God is with us

Now the birth of Jesus Christ took place in this way. When his mother Mary had been betrothed to Joseph, before they came together she was found to be with child of the Holy Spirit; and her husband Joseph, being a just man and unwilling to put her to shame, resolved to divorce her quietly. But as he considered this, behold, an angel of the Lord appeared to him in a dream, saying 'Joseph, son of David, do not fear to take Mary your wife, for that which is conceived in her is of the Holy Spirit; she will bear a son, and you shall call his name Jesus, for he will save his people from their sins'. All this took place to fulfil what the Lord had spoken by the prophet: 'Behold, a virgin shall conceive and bear a son, and his name shall be called Emmanuel' (which means, God with us). When Joseph awoke from sleep, he did as the angel of the Lord commanded him; he took his wife [back] (Matthew 1. 18-24).

We might ask why Matthew, in contrast to Luke, portrays Joseph and not Mary as the one who receives God's news about the birth of the Saviour of the people of Israel. We might ask what Joseph's motives are

27

(for they are not clear from the text) for wanting to divorce his wife. We could once again pose the question (very popular recently) of the historical formulation used here to describe the virgin birth, and its significance for our faith. We might consider the meaning of giving a name and the significance of the name Jesus – 'the Lord saves'. We might ask what the prophet originally intended by the quotation from Isaiah 7. 14, whose meaning here is highly controversial. But those are questions outside the scope of this short meditation.

Here we are concerned with the name 'Emmanuel', the announcement that 'God is with us' through this Jesus.

One connotation of 'God is with us' that is not superficial or erroneous, is worth noting. When we say that man as a created being is certainly concerned with God, that God is the Lord and goal of man, that without him there is no meaning to our life, that he is our helper and saviour, on whose gracious providence we are dependent, that he of his mercy will forgive us our guilt, that we shall have to plead our responsibility before his court of judgment, that for those who believe in, hope in and love him, he prepares an eternal life of happiness, then we have interpreted 'God is with us' in the right way and in a number of its aspects. It would be a wonderful blessing if all men were to realize that interpretation of 'God is with us' in their lives. All those explanations are ultimately directed in hope to the one deeper mystery of 'God is with us'.

But none of them reaches the absolute Christian understanding of 'God with us'. If we said that God was close to us only in his finite gifts, in placing us as creative beings in our own reality, and guiding that reality to its immanent fulfilment through the forgiveness of our guilt and the final validation of our own mature existence; if we said that God himself was close to us only insofar as all these created human realities came from him and referred to him and prompted us to refer to him in acknowledgment and thankful, prayerful love; then we should misunderstand the radical nature of the Christian understanding of 'God with us'.

God himself is with us. God himself is with us through himself and not merely through the mediation of finite gifts to a finite creation. Scripture and tradition testify to the highly-nuanced nature of the ultimate mystery of our existence: namely, that God communicates himself to us in his own infinite and inconceivable reality. He gives us his own Spirit, who sounds the profundity of the Godhead, God's own inward life. Thus the Father and Son come to reside in us, just as the Son is one with the Father from eternity. We share in the divine nature; we are no longer mere servants but truly God's children born of God. We shall see and love God not in the glass and likeness of creaturely mediation but directly, face to face. Traditional theology speaks therefore − lest the radical nature of this biblical teaching be diminished subsequently − of uncreated grace, of the fact that direct perception of God is not mediated by a created reality, from which God would then have to be recognized. Classical theology speaks of the direct indwelling of the threefold God in man, of the self-communication of God.

At first all that may sound rather abstract. But it is the ultimate truth about mankind, whether we have already reached it and realized it in the banality of our everyday existence or not. Because we are finite beings, when we live from ourselves alone we succumb to an almost irresistible inclination to think quite finitely of ourselves and of our fulfilment. We tend to be falsely unassuming, to be satisfied with the visible and tangible. If it were a matter of our own perspective alone, we would be quite right to be content with a finite happiness. Every sin in the world, because it posits a finite good as absolute, testifies to that false contentment to which we may not resign ourselves. We are forbidden to do so not only by a law of external origin, one that remains alien to us, but by the fact that God in his very boundlessness, in the sovereignty of his mercy and loving kindness, has already made himself the innermost law of our nature, before we become conscious of ourselves and fear to let ourselves fall into that inconceivable infinity which already fulfils us from the innermost core of our being, and we take shelter in the finite margins of our existence and try to find happiness there. The statement that God is with us (as Christians understand it absolutely) says that we cannot be immoderate enough in that thirst that God himself has given us; in our craving for freedom, happiness, the closeness of love, knowledge, peace and ultimate fulfilment. Any guilty immoderacy in our lives, if we consider it closely, is only that lack of control which posits a finite reality as absolutely necessary for our own happiness. A man like that is guilty because he does not dare to make the believing, hoping, loving leap into the inconceivability and unrestrictedness of his true happiness, which consists only of the incomprehensibility of God.

The abstract interpretation which I have offered of the 'God with us' of the text in question, is not so distant as it at first seems. It seems so because we are distant from our own 'supernature', which is God himself. Whenever we hear in ourselves the infinite claim and summons of existence (which is already inwardly blessed) accepting no more conditions and limitations apart from the fact that we are the beginning but not the fulfilled infinity; whenever there is a will to unconditional love which opens out to others in a way that must incur the danger of mortal self-denial; wherever in the fall towards the mortal darkness of death we still believe that that experience is finite and that the hope of everlasting life is infinite; in those and many other basic events of human existence, we experience the hope and belief that God himself — and no finite thing — is the fulfilment of all finite human being.

That is the meaning of 'uncreated grace'. It is a grace mediated by Jesus Christ, yet it is at work in all world history and human history as its innermost realization of what it is potentially. Therefore it is the innermost core of all human existence.

But the doctrine of 'uncreated grace' indicates more than an unutterable bliss as the future of mankind. With it we reach the ultimate gravity of the Christian notion of man. This God who is 'God with us' in that way is not only the illimitable mystery that remains absolute mystery even in direct apprehension of God, and thus can be borne by human perception only if that perception is itself fulfilled in the love which alone makes it possible for God who is love to be perceived as greater than one's own heart (with its craving for enlightenment). This 'God with us' is not only the God of absolute freedom (of decisions which can no longer be negated, and arrangements which can only be endured and accepted in the unconditional surrender of love which loves this divine freedom as such). It is rather the incredible closeness of God which gives Christian 'morality' its ultimate radicality. Many thousands of reversals occur in human history and in an individual's life which are wrong by the yardstick of the very nature of man and his finite world; they are, therefore, objectively refused by human morality, but do not really cancel the ultimate affirmative relationship to this God who gives himself and is so inconceivably close to us. (There are many 'objective sins' which imply no 'subjective guilt' and therefore do not stand in the way of salvation — that is how scholastic theology would put it). Repeatedly, however, human freedom (acting on the material of worldly morality) offers a No to that God of absolute closeness, without, however, specifically formulating it like that. Then we have sin ('grave sin') in the Christian sense. Sin is not only saying No to the objective structure of man and the world, and therefore to the commandments of the God who wills those structures (but only with the will that accords with the conditional and finite nature of those structures); it is saying No to God himself in his absolute closeness to us. It is the No of human freedom denying itself the absolute venture of the love of God and its own love.

It is both terrible and comforting to dwell in the inconceivable nearness of God, and so to be loved by God himself that the first and last gift is infinity and inconceivability itself. But we have no choice. God is with us.

PART TWO

5 The power of birth

Where can we find a way into the mystery of Christmas to suit us now, at this time? That is the first question. We find a way to the mystery of Jesus' birth if we come to it from the experience of real life, approaching it so to speak 'from below'. By 'below' I mean life below, where we are, and where we experience ourselves as we are: both our own life and the life of Jesus himself. I mean 'way' both in human terms and in terms of what biblical scholars and theologians call 'ascent Christology'. To take the answer further: Access to Christmas is also to be sought and found in the perspective of Jesus' cross and Easter. The beginning is revealed from the viewpoint of the end; ultimately, it is revealed only thus; the beginning is the beginning of the end. We should also remember, of course, the traditional Christian interpretation of the Christmas mystery as the descent of God into the history of the world and men, and as God's epiphany in his own majesty. Finally, we should not forget to talk of Christmas in terms of Christ in us today, and therefore of how we live the mystery of Christmas in faith, hope and love.

Experience with Jesus; experience with ourselves

Today we have to find a way into the mystery of
Christmas by starting from life itself, which is our own
and therefore Jesus' life (in spite of its uniqueness and
difference from our own life). What does that mean?
The Church has of course always followed that path,
beginning with the first experiences of Jesus' first disciples with Jesus, then in the Christologies of the
New Testament, right up to the Christological Councils
of Ephesus and Chalcedon in the fifth century, and the
later dogmatic teachings which were based on those
Councils and which, in terms of the official doctrine of
the Church, added hardly anything to the conciliar
pronouncements. That way is, as it were, taken for
granted; therefore the traditional Christmas sermon
doesn't start with that quiet and careful prelude, but
begins straight away with a great organ-loud proclamation of the descent of the Father's eternal Son from his
eternal glory pre-existing all history, into the world and
into history, and into our 'flesh'. God became man and
dwelled among us.

That is usually the first way of putting it at Christmas. And even if we wanted to preach a Christian
sermon in the style of what is known as 'descent Christology' and to talk immediately of the crucified God, of
the fact that the everlasting God descended into the
impasses of our flesh, our history and the darkness of
our death, we should by no means have avoided the
difficulty and perplexity of the message of the descent
and Incarnation of God. That message to some extent
embarrasses and disturbs us when we first hear it
today; if we take ourselves and it seriously it is difficult
to understand. What can it mean when we say that the
eternal Word in which the eternal God, the Father,
expresses himself for himself from all eternity and is
with himself, became man? He who is the all-penetrat-

THE POWER OF BIRTH

ing, all-positing, all-maintaining primal round of that inconceivably large universe of matter, life and mind which we think of today as continuously evolving? Isn't that God both too close to everything and too distant from it, so that it seems more appropriate to think of him almost as in a Greek myth than as taking the form of a human being on the small, lost planet which we call Earth? Even if — as a last resort, despite Christian teaching properly understood, and almost involuntarily — we could explain this God satisfactorily (as far as we are concerned) by saying that he merely put on human clothing, what use is that notion to us in the harsh reality of our everyday life, if that divine adventure took place a long time past in some small corner of space and time, in the infinitesimal history we elevate to the level of universal history, and if that God long ago disappeared again into a distant, silent inconceivability?

Finally, if we really wish to understand the message of Christmas, we have to begin where this history of salvation and faith really began: in the experience which people really had of Jesus in Jesus' own environment, and to which, in order to have that experience at all, they contributed their own experience of themselves as human beings. First and foremost, those people did not experience God or a God in a human form through which the divine splendour shone overwhelmingly from the start. They experienced a man as they were men; a man with a human beginning, with an historically conditioned nature, with a normal life tending relentlessly towards death; a man who spoke their language, who basically and unaffectedly accepted his social and religious situation, who felt and lived like all men of his world, who in his religious preaching talked in the religious concepts and imagery of his time, who talked and kept his counsel, rejoiced and wept, and lived and died, whom others called Rabbi, whom people could embrace, whose peculiarities could be displeasing and incomprehensible, whose words did not seem from the start necessarily to be set far above all other human wisdom. And the fact that his life ended in a death which was not only the ultimate disaster of his physical life but also the cold hard failure of the mission which he had undertaken; that would be merely to underline the experience that this was a man living with the unresolved problematic nature proper to men.

Jesus was a man, a true man without reservation, and without anything left out, a man like us. Everything we can learn about him allows us to interpret and understand him from the viewpoint of human experience (our own experience of ourselves: poor, heavy-laden, helplessly perplexed and dying mortals). Therefore it is clear from the start that, if Jesus is an answer, he can only be an answer to the question and perplexity which we ourselves are by being so in that same human way. Autocratically, desperately, we may not diminish the question which we are and which we take to him. We must accept ourselves as a question in his questioning as it actually is in its absoluteness; as a quest for and question about that mystery we call God; as a question both of unassuaged desperation and of absolute hope at one and the same time.

Birth, the beginning of a history

Before we meditate further on these points, we have to formulate our intermediate result more exactly. If it is to become meaningful for us, Christmas has to begin with the experience of Jesus as a true man, with an experience of him from below, with an experience of the human Jesus part of whose substance and criterion has to be the experience we have of ourselves.

The message of Christmas is first and foremost news of a birth, the beginning of a human being. Jesus' birth, his beginning, has to be understood from the basis of Jesus' *life* and death as the destiny of a man, though, of course, a quite specific man. Insofar as his life and death, in that they reveal his birth, can only be understood from the viewpoint of the uniqueness of his dying into the finality of God's saving love – from the uniqueness of his redeemed death, which we call 'Resurrection' – the uniqueness and the ultimate meaning of his birth are only revealed through his death and his Resurrection. We shall now consider the essential nature of Jesus' birth from the viewpoint of his life as a whole.

Here we must make a double, human and theological, presupposition. Of course a human life is the story of a freedom which creatively shapes a life, and not only the enforced unfolding and therefore explication of what a man already possesses when he sets out on his life. It is also not merely a physically inescapable explication of the internal and external biological, social and historical premises of an individual life.

Human freedom acts from a given, determined and finite inward and outward situation which prevails throughout life, irrespective of whether freedom accepts or protests against what it makes of that situation – the law, that is, according to which freedom occurred. A history of freedom reveals the beginning; the beginning can be seen from life and its completion.

That is all the more true when we consider not only the human but the theological presupposition involved here: all human life, without injury to its freedom, is encompassed and supported by the knowledge and will of God, who ordains and posits the beginning out of his own will that it should reach its end and goal. A life and its fulfilment reveal what the beginning already bore in embryo within it; life and completion reveal the beginning intended by God and wanted by God and determined by him as proceeding towards that quite definite end; they reveal God's plan for this life, which is not merely, so to speak, a definition of this life revolving in God's head, but the real inward uniqueness of that beginning. Life and its end explicate the beginning as it is ordained, planned and intended by God.

Christianity has therefore rightly followed the New Testament in working from the life and fulfilment of Jesus back to his beginning: his conception and birth. It has seen his birth as that of the one whom he revealed himself to be in his life. The legitimacy of looking back from a life to its beginning is not questioned by the fact that in the New Testament (this was more or less discarded in later Christology) other events in Jesus' life which reveal the entire and original meaning of his whole life for us in a special way are understood as embryonic pointers to what Jesus ultimately is. Hence, for instance, his baptism or Resurrection is seen as causally related to his divine Sonship.

Such assertions tend to simplify matters by joining the history of Jesus' reality in itself to the history of our understanding of the same reality. Such propositions, though permissible on that count, do not remove the justification for referring back to the beginning of Jesus' life. Such a beginning should not be understood as a self-contained event, but as the beginning of an evolving history oriented from the start to those points at which it is strikingly revealed as what it is, so that the will of God in regard to the beginning was always an aspect of what he willed for life as a whole and its main events.

What does Jesus' life say about his birth?

What can we say about that beginning, about Jesus'
birth, if that birth is to be understood from the viewpoint of his life, but may not as yet be interpreted
explicitly from the viewpoint of his death and Resurrection (the theme of the next section of this meditation)? What does his life have to say about his birth?

We must certainly ask what his life (of which his
word is of course part) says about Jesus, if we ignore
his death as redeemed by his Resurrection. Jesus, (understood historically) did not merely understand and explain his activity and proclamation as unambiguously
oriented from the start to his death, and, in his human,
objectifying and reflective consciousness, did not
reckon from the start on the capsizing of his life's
work by a violent death brought about by the religious
and political powers of his immediate world. If we
inquire into his birth from the viewpoint of his life,
if we attempt a Christology from below, from the
empirical aspect of his human life, and try to define
his birth from that point, we are of course attempting a
very difficult task. We have to take into account the
fact that in the synoptic gospels, those words of Jesus
which in the proclamation of the Kingdom of God
maintain and express a specific self-understanding of
Jesus, are already co-determined by the knowledge of
the earliest Christians about the full and entire reality
of Jesus; by a knowledge that this earliest form of
Christianity was only possible by virtue of the experience of the cross and the Resurrection of Jesus. When,
in order to understand his birth, we inquire into Jesus'
life, of which his proclamation forms a constituent part,
then it is obvious that a very short meditation can only
concentrate on essentials.

The Word of God entered the world

To answer the question tentatively, we can say: in Jesus' life, person and proclamation seen as a whole, we find the ultimate, irreversible and of itself victorious word of forgiving and liberating self-communication of God to us in historical tangibility. Therefore this word of God, because it is inseparable from the person of Jesus, entered into his birth into the world: the irrevocable word of God to us in which God grants himself to us ultimately as forgiveness, liberation and deification. This proposition does not deny but presupposes that that word, which is Jesus himself, reaches its ultimate validity and confirmation in what we call Jesus' Resurrection. But the Resurrection was already ordained in Jesus' life.

If we try to explain this preliminary proposition, it is clear that we cannot give a detailed account of the historico-exegetical and biblical-theological material needed to explain it, but have to speak very summarily. It is also clear that our consideration of Jesus' life should focus above all on his proclamation and his self-interpretation, which are the essential substance of his life, even though the final confirmation of his teaching and his self-understanding comes from Easter.

Jesus' self-consciousness

If, to interpret his birth, we look at Jesus' life historically, though on a modest scale, we can affirm that Jesus had a human self-consciousness though one which may not be identical in Monophysite style with the consciousness of the divine *Logos*, as though it and the entire reality of Jesus were ultimately passively controlled, put on therefore like a uniform, by the sole active divine Subject. Jesus' human self-consciousness was at that distance from the God whom he called his Father that is proper to a created being: he was free, and yet obedient; he worshipped and yielded to God's inconceivability like any other human consciousness.

Quite apart from an essential selfness, maintained throughout a lifetime, the selfness, that is, of a profound non-reflexive consciousness of being radically and uniquely close to God (as is apparent from the special nature of his behaviour towards the 'Father'), the self-objectifying and verbalizing (self-)consciousness of Jesus also has a history. It works up to the horizon of understanding and shares in the ideas of Jesus' environment, not 'condescendingly', for others, but so that he himself becomes part of that environment. Jesus' consciousness learns and makes new, surprising experiences; it is threatened by the ultimate crises of self-identification, even if those crises, no less acute because of it, are subject to an awareness that they too remain hidden in the will of the 'Father'. His relationship to the Father, which is given (and only thus given) in that consciousness, is something that Jesus objectifies and verbalizes for himself and for his audience by means of what is often known as 'imminent expectation' − the news of a new and ultimate imminence of the Kingdom of God. It is customary, of course, to see that as meaning a short chronological interval before the coming of the Kingdom of God, and to make that short interval the decisive point of that expectation. Jesus, however, rejects that viewpoint and yet announces an imminent expectation of the Kingdom of God.

If we play down the question that Jesus finally left open: namely, that of the ultimate meaning of the 'nearness' of the coming Day of Yahweh, because this 'nearness' of his proclamation on the one hand and the knowledge of the obscurity of the day on the other hand, as they existed in Jesus' consciousness, cannot be synthesized into a higher unity, it is permissible to speak of an 'error' in Jesus' imminent expectation. In such an 'error' he merely shared our lot, because to err in that way is better for man in history (and therefore for Jesus too) than to know everything already, and thereby to forgo the darkness and anguish of a situation of trial and decision undertaken in the spirit of hope.

But if we should presuppose a notion of 'error' which is more appropriate to the nature of human existence, there is no reason to speak of Jesus' making a mistake in his imminent expectation.. A genuine human consciousness *must* have an unknown future in front of it. The imminent expectation that Jesus verbalized in chronological terms was the right way for him. It was the way offered him by his situation to understand the closeness of God calling him to make an unconditional decision. Only an enthusiast for a false and unhistorical kind of existentialism or idealism who thinks that he is able to decide for or against God (in some situation beyond history), is really surprised at this objective translation of the facts governing a decision about salvation into the form of 'imminent expectations'. That is the case, even if other people (for instance, we of the twentieth century) have to (and ought to) translate this poignant new situation of the choice about salvation into different objective terms.

The core of Jesus' proclamation

Jesus' proclamation of an imminent expectation of the Kingdom of God has, therefore, to be interpreted correctly. In it he proclaims the closeness of the Kingdom as the situation of absolute decision for absolute salvation or its opposite as given 'now' and only now. But in Jesus' proclamation this situation is so constituted that God offers *salvation* and nothing else to all men as sinners; God, therefore, does not merely set up a situation which is permanently ambivalent as far as human freedom is concerned, but decides this through his own action in favour of man's salvation, without thus dispensing man from his own free responsibility for his salvation. Jesus does not unite the proclamation of the triumphant existence of the Kingdom of forgiveness for sinners by God himself with a call to free conversion in men, in a 'system' comprehensible to man outside his attitude of acceptance in hope. That may be justifiably described as the historically perceived core of Jesus' message. The rest of his message can be understood only from that basis: his struggle against the dominance of a law that sets itself in God's place; against all legalism and the absolute elevation of religious or secular powers in the world; against any merely pious morality, such as a justification by works which tries to set itself up against God.

If (and insofar as) the proclamation of the absolute nearness of the Kingdom of God in the foregoing sense constitutes the core of Jesus' message, it is true to say that Jesus proclaims the Kingdom of God and not himself.

This man Jesus is (authentically) man (pure and simple), because he forgets himself for the sake of God and men who are in need of salvation, and exists only in that particular state of self-oblivion. A pronouncement about himself by Jesus (which of course exists) is therefore only conceivable when and because it occurs as an inevitable aspect of the closeness of God proclaimed by Jesus in his own self-occurrence. Jesus' 'function' reveals his 'nature'.

This nearness of God is the closeness of the salvation which God himself ordains in the continuing freedom of man. It is not to be conceived as existing in Jesus' consciousness as a given and uniform situation; it is not an already universally given human existential which can at most be forgotten and suppressed, and for that reason only has to be preached anew. For Jesus that nearness of God is with him and his preaching in a new, unique and henceforth insurpassable way.

Why that is the case for Jesus, and (according to the preaching of the pre-Easter Jesus) independently of his death and his Resurrection (which of course considerably enlighten and resolve this question in another way) is not easy to say. Is Jesus in that preaching expressing no more than his unique relation to God, which he does not find in others, but wants to mediate to them, as far as they are capable of receiving it? Would the Kingdom come 'quickly', and in its full glory, if Jesus' message were not rejected? Did Jesus 'have to' preach on that hypothesis?

In the end we have to say of this whole problem that Jesus' rejection, death and Resurrection help us to place it appropriately. Ultimately, we cannot and must not ignore Jesus' end and fulfilment; we cannot expect a straightforward resolution of the problem.

Conversely, however, Jesus' preaching of the nearness of the Kingdom of God (given only with him) is our own decision situation (now). It is also true for us in spite of our – still uncertain – dependence on a still extensive human history. Through that preaching, at least insofar as it is confirmed by Jesus' death and Resurrection, we have an absolute decision-situation, for we enjoy an offer of salvation from God, which did not exist before Jesus. In any case, an individual can never put himself in the situation of mankind as a whole.

The newly-proclaimed nearness of the Kingdom of God

This nearness of the Kingdom of God was not always given but is only given 'now' and newly in Jesus. As the intrinsically victorious salvific situation of definitively converted man, that nearness, as far as the pre-Easter Jesus is concerned, is indissolubly connected with his own person. We can now see the connexion of the foregoing with Christmas, when we try to understand the mystery of the feast 'from below', from the viewpoint of the life of Jesus considered as an historically perceptible event. The thesis of the indissoluble unity between Jesus' message of the nearness of the Kingdom of God and his person is a matter for exegetes; it is however tenable in terms of modern exegesis.

I have spoken of an indissoluble connexion between the imminence of the Kingdom of God proclaimed as something new by Jesus *and* his 'person'. More exactly: the pre-Easter Jesus holds that new nearness of the Kingdom will occur *through* his proclamation of that very nearness.

It is now easier to understand how Jesus could identify the Kingdom of God with himself in that way, before his death and his Resurrection were allotted a place in (his) theology. It is also easier to understand why the significant core of his preaching was this Kingdom of God and not, directly, himself.

Of course the new imminence of the Kingdom of God preached by Jesus as something new and not yet given, is not merely a relatively greater degree of imminence than hitherto, which itself could be exceeded and therefore dissolved by an even greater nearness and urgency of God's call. Such an idea of Jesus' function, corresponding to that of any prophet who always knows that he will be replaced by others, who will preach another, new word of God, is rendered impossible by Jesus' imminent expectation. He is the last call of God after which no other is to come or can come on account of the definitive nature of the self-communication of God (who represents himself in no other way) in the declaration that the power of divine mercy essentially constitutes this self-communication of God in the freedom of men.

But this thesis isn't exactly easy to understand. It does not degrade Jesus to the status of any prophet or religious ranter. Why is the givenness of that which is proclaimed (the nearness of the Kingdom of God) dependent on Jesus' preaching? Perhaps it is because otherwise we would know nothing of what is proclaimed and then it would not be so effective, since what isn't known can't be accepted in human freedom? But if that were the answer, we would have to explain how and why, without this proclamation by this particular Jesus, we would know nothing about what is proclaimed: namely the nearness of the Kingdom of God.

What is more, *in what* would the new, insurpassable imminence of the Kingdom of God consist, if it were there, not explicitly without Jesus' proclamation, but of itself, independent of Jesus' proclamation? How could we explain, in terms of Jesus' religious experience, that is, the fact that he knows about an imminence of God's coming as something radically new, if he tells the ignorant only what did not indeed exist before this proclamation, but would have happened quite independently of it? When, where — in other words — can Jesus have learned what he knew?

Jesus new unique relationship to God

If we consider carefully the notion of a purely gnoseological necessity of Jesus' preaching of the Kingdom, we must confess that he did not preach anything really new, but only, even though in a prophetically definitive style, proclaimed the old news in a new way. In fact his originality is often questioned. That is justifiable if we overlook the fact that his preaching proclaims a hitherto non-existent and therefore radically new nearness of God which is present only through his, Jesus', preaching. Looked at soberly, there is no more to say than that: Jesus experienced a relationship to God which on the one hand (in comparison to other men) he experienced uniquely and in a new way, and which on the other hand he looked on as exemplary for other men in their relationship to God. He experienced his unique and new 'filial relationship' to the 'Father' as meaningful for all men, inasmuch as in it, as far as all men were concerned, God's movement towards them occurred in a new and irrevocable way.

In this unique and, as far as we are concerned, exemplary relationship to God, the pre-Easter Jesus is able to experience the imminence of the Kingdom of God in his person. Thus he knows that the coming of the Kingdom is indissolubly bound up with his preaching and is, in fact, his very preaching.

Through his death and Resurrection, of course, all the foregoing is ultimately (and only then ultimately) rendered definitive in itself and for us. But we now understand how Jesus was able, even before Easter, to recognize and experience himself as the absolute bringer of salvation, even if that self-interpretation obtains its ultimate credibility (as far as we are concerned) from Easter, and only then is revealed in its ultimate profundity. In himself Jesus experiences that absolute, triumphant turning of God to himself which had not existed previously in that way among 'sinners', and perceives it to be meaningful, valid and irreversible for all men. The pre-Easter Jesus, too, in terms proper to his own self-understanding, was already proclaiming the Kingdom of God, as it had not existed historically before, and as it was there *through* and *in* him.

God's definitive word to the world

Now we are, I think, in a position to say how we should understand Christmas, Jesus' beginning and birth, in the perspective of Jesus' life. Christmas is the birth of the 'Son' of the eternal God. When we say 'Son', perhaps we have not yet said expressly and in ecclesiological or official credal terms what the Christmas dogma proclaims when it asserts the descent of the eternal Word of the Father, of the Son pure and simple, into history, and into our flesh.

If what has been said about the self-understanding of the pre-Easter Jesus is correct, then Jesus is, in a unique and insurpassable way, the Son of the eternal God. He is not to be degraded to the level of a prophetic figure, a mere religious genius, or a salvationist. In his life and his proclamation, Jesus is in person the ultimate and insurpassable Word of God to the world. We might object that one word does not mean much, because it 'only' includes the God-given triumphant mercy of God, which encompasses history as a whole with all its guilt and stumbling, and expresses God himself as the absolute human future.

But if this all-encompassing Word has also to be filled with all the words of God and answers of men which occur in the whole of human history, then this open and (in the above-mentioned respect) eternal Word is definitive, because it communicates to history as a whole its coming in God's inconceivable glory. Hence it cannot be surpassed. All history to come, and all its unforseeable individual futures, are at work in this Word, yet cannot lead beyond it. It is the Word of the absolute, all-reconciling future-containing God himself, and not something merely preliminary to God.

If Jesus in his person, in the unity with God from which he speaks, and if his word is that Word, and if that Word is pronounced by God (because it can be said only by God), then Jesus one and entire is pronounced from eternity as the intentionally triumphant self-communication of God to God's world. From the beginning of his existence he is intended by God as that Word, even when that Word, in order to be and to be heard by us, had to unfold and expound in a human history. Christians are right to say that this Word of God, in which God communicated himself in his ulttimate definitive nature and in an historically perceptible manner, was born at Christmas.

A Christology which begins from below with the experience of the real Jesus and his message, will, as the New Testament writings testify, return to Jesus' birth. Jesus, as the one who shows himself later, had to be intended unconditionally from eternity by God. That must be so, if he is not merely a man who still stands before the open question (for himself and for us): whether union with God succeeds in freedom or fails in guilt. Jesus must be a man in whom God's triumph becomes an event in human freedom. Even in a Christology from below, Christmas is the coming of God's Word to us, its entry into the world. Christmas is the word through which God communicates himself in reconciliation.

6 Obedient unto death

Our 'Christology from below', from the viewpoint of 'the life of Jesus', becomes quite comprehensible if we look back at Christmas from the cross and from Jesus' Resurrection. In the framework of these meditations it would of course be inappropriate to try to work out a satisfactory theology of Jesus' cross and Resurrection, or to justify in fundamental theological terms our Yes of faith to the Resurrection. All I can do here is to offer a few indications to show more clearly how the cross and Resurrection put in a radical perspective what I have hitherto said about Christmas from the viewpoint of Jesus' life; the cross and the Resurrection, so to speak, confirm what has been said: they set God's seal on it.

But how does that word of God come to us in history, so that history continues on its way, and is not already cancelled and fulfilled in the ultimate self-revelation of God, in God's definitive Kingdom, in glory, and in the direct beatific vision of the God of eternity? How does the word of God's self-surrender come to us? In spite of its givenness within a continuing history, God himself offers his word to us tangibly and irrevocably. But how is that paradox possible?

God's word — man's answer

We can say with certainty that if God's word is directed to human freedom and is not to cancel that freedom, it must be fully united with man's free answer in which he accepts God's self-communication of God, which is a human and a divine act at one and the same time. If that were not so, God's only offer of himself which we would know would be such that we would never know if it was really accepted. In that case, we would not know whether God's self-offer had prevailed of itself and surpassed ambivalent human freedom to the advantage of that freedom.

God's word has to be issued to us in the free obedience of a man to God, in which, in one man, God's promise is also perceptible for us; the promise, in other words, that God's mercy includes our freedom despite the ambivalent attitude of our freedom to its own salvation. Of course we may not conclude that we need do no more to be saved; that we could avoid our own freely-chosen obedience in regard to God's offer of himself. This necessary word of God's self-communication to mankind in a single human being has to be a union of God's word and man's answer as well as (we dare to add) God's acceptance of that answer.

God's word has another unique feature, in the foregoing perspective at least: man's obedient answer must form part of that word as something worked by God. But does this answer appear as it is in human history, in man's nature as that nature is constituted and as we understand it, so that it encompasses man as a whole and is given an ultimate and supremely valid answer? The only possible reply is that the answer has to be given through death. The fortunate response which is accepted by God and yet is something we can experience is what we call resurrection.

Submission to God

That answer should encompass the whole man; it must also be an ultimate and definitive response. Unconditionally, without any reservation, men must yield to God himself, as he is in himself, and as he is in his illimitable freedom. But that kind of complete lack of reservation is possible only in death. In death the individual loses everything. In death he abandons everything including himself; he loses his freedom and all his individual potentialities wholly and completely, provided of course that he does not think of death as an absolute protest against everything that is taken from him, because it is taken from him, and in his last guilty hopelessness interprets this process as a supremely meaningless event.

If, therefore, in death (and in the end that is the only place where it is possible), a man submits purely and simply, unconditionally and obediently to God as the One who gives himself (and nothing else but himself) to man as man's absolute future beyond all particular things within this world of ours; and if the union of that gift and its acceptance seems to us to be valid (in what we call 'resurrection' and the 'experience of resurrection'), then for us too that is God's triumphant bestowal of himself upon us. It is so because Jesus, who died and rose again in that process, identified himself from the start with a message of God's forgiving self-communication to *us*, and therefore in his death and Resurrection is indeed that promise to us.

Life and death as destiny

This is not the place to elucidate the foregoing in greater detail or to try to prove that Jesus' Resurrection is credible. But if we presuppose that it is possible, we can say: The Crucified and Risen Jesus is God's insurpassable and ultimate self-bestowal upon us in mercy and loving kindness. That self-bestowal rises out of God to consume all our equivocation and all our sinfulness. In his death and Resurrection Jesus finally became, in a way which we can grasp, God's self-gift to us, which he already was, most profoundly, in his life and in his preaching of the new and ultimate closeness of God to us in the proclamation of the Kingdom.

In that perspective we can now look back at Christmas in a new way. From the viewpoint of that profundity, Christmas is something posited by God himself in sovereign triumph in Jesus: Christmas is the onset of his death and Resurrection. Whatever additional detail may emerge from an inquiry into the problem of whether and how Jesus in his objective and linguistically competent consciousness may have been aware of his death as something protected by God's power; and the problem whether and how in that regard Jesus' earthly consciousness may have reached a clearer understanding of his destiny in death, his destiny in life nevertheless proceeds from God's sovereign ordinance (which intends Jesus' entire destiny essentially as God's bestowal of himself upon us) towards that death. Implicitly at least, Jesus had always accepted that death in virtue of his unconditional obedience to God's decree. Towards the end of his life, Jesus expressly and decisively accepted his death as a prophetic fate. Therefore Christmas is really the beginning of the fulfilment in which Jesus, unconditionally and without support from anything other than God, cast himself into the inconceivability of God as his own fulfilment, a fulfilment he himself did not ordain.

Christmas is the beginning of the man who — for us too — was to die in this culminating act of faithful obedience. That was also the case inasmuch as human

55

death itself, as the act of trusting and hoping freedom, does not occur simply in the moment of medical mortality, but constitutes the innermost structure of an entire human life which, in all self-abandonment, in all disappointments, anguish and failure, works towards that all-encompassing and yet hoping abandonment that we are accustomed to call death.

When we stand in faith before the Child's crib, we have to see that it is here that the decline called death begins, that descent which alone saves because its emptiness is filled with the unutterable inconceivability of God, which alone answers all the questions posed by our life in a thousand little ways. It answers them by surpassing them. Of course the death referred to here is always death redeemed by God, death fulfilled by God, which in our perspective is the descent of our existence and in God's perspective the ascent of God in what we call the Resurrection. Christmas is the beginning of that redeemed death and in any real sense can be understood only in that light.

The light of Christmas and the angels' carolling in praise of God, and their proclamation to men of an ultimate reconciliation through the grace of God must shine and resound in the depths of our death, or they will not be seen or heard. Christmas is not a feast of consolation that rescues us for a few uplifting moments from an incomprehensible fate. We celebrate Christmas where we are alive, in our movement towards death, and we do that because Jesus' birth was the beginning of his death.

7 God made man

We must not forget the view of the Christmas mystery which is already apparent in the New Testament, and which looks down on to Christmas and says 'And the Word was made flesh'.

That almost two-thousand-year-old church meditation is essentially identical with the full Christian and ecclesiological teaching on the Trinitarian nature of the eternal God, the 'Incarnation' of the eternal Logos, and the 'hypostatic union' of the eternal, pre-existent Son of the Father with a fully human reality having a body and a soul; with, therefore, a human 'nature' in time.

If Jesus is the historical, unique and irrevocable communication of God in his human reality, with history, body and soul, and a personal human freedom in his life and death, and if this self-communication of God means God himself and not merely a gift which is distinct from him (in being created and finite), and if we do not conceive such finite gifts of God as having a saving effect for us; if there is no doubt whatsoever that this self-communication of God is a matter of God himself as he is in and for himself; and if he gives himself to us thus and in Jesus, then a unique and definitive union exists in Jesus between him and God: a unity given from the beginning (even though it must of course unfold in such a way that we have to say, straightforwardly and resolutely: In Jesus, for him and through him for us there is God whole and irrevocable: God as himself – though of course as the Inconceivable and Nameless. God himself is represented in no other way. That of course appears in the traditional doctrinal formulas of the Councils of Ephesus and Chalcedon in the fifth century, which taught that the eternal Logos of the Father took up the entire, undiminished and free human reality of Jesus as his own and united it with himself, so that this reality, without any reduction of autonomy and freedom, even in regard to God, became the reality and manifestation of God as he is in himself.

Eternal Son of the Father

In this sense, Christian dogma states boldly that Jesus 'is' 'God' and the 'eternal Son of the Father'; that his human reality in birth, life, death and ultimate fulness can and must be asserted of God himself; and that the characteristics of God can and must be asserted of Jesus.

Of course in such statements of fact, and in such divine and human predications of the one God man Jesus, and in accordance with official church teaching, we have to add that this 'factuality' has a significance that makes it essentially different from similar factual statements in and about our everyday world. In normal circumstances (for instance, Peter is a man), it is a question of plain identity between subject and predicate. In the Christological statements, however, we are faced with a mysterious unity of God and Jesus in which all the divine and the human reality may no longer be conceived as identically the same, because they are not so, but remain 'unmixed' — as the Council of Chalcedon stresses.

That must always be taken into consideration in the attribution of divine predicates to Jesus; when, for instance, we say: God was born, God died, or Mary is the mother of God. If we forget that absolute difference in this mysterious unity of God and man in Jesus, we are not more faithful or pious, but heretical; we are in fact Monophysites.

God's 'influence' on Jesus

We must think of the way in which the divine sovereign freedom of God ordains the man Jesus and his freedom as set over against us. If we wanted to think of this 'influence' of God on Jesus in freedom in some other way (in the way, for instance, in which a higher principle of control in us permeates the lower levels and dimensions of our reality), then we would (in the formulation of traditional Christology) turn from the divine and the human reality to a (complex) single 'nature'. We should then be Monophysites and Mono- thelites. We should be heretics. If, in contradistinction to traditional Christological terminology, we think of an active centre of freedom with a free finite personality of the kind appropriate to human being, set at an in- finite distance from God, and use the term 'person' in a human sense, then of course Jesus has a created human personality; in that sense he is a human 'person'.

To assert the opposite would be erroneous; in fact that belief is rejected by the Church as Monophysitism, a rejection emphasized in the condemnation of Mono- theletism; of the belief, in other words, that only a single active centre of freedom exists as the mysterious unity of God and man in the one Jesus whole and entire.

God in Jesus

When we speak of the one, single divine 'person' in Jesus in traditional church terminology, then we refer to God, insofar as he accepts and encompasses the wholly 'personal' reality of the authentic man Jesus, without cancelling it, so that it really becomes God's being among us, the irrevocable Word of God's acceptance in himself for us.

We need not deny that the traditional Christological statements of the Chruch's magisterium, which we use at Christmas, repeating the formulas of one and a half thousand years, in order to proclaim the mystery of Christmas, can also be misunderstood and are in fact (though without any guilt) wrongly understood by Christians; by which I mean that they are understood in a Monophysite sense. Christians and non-Christians rightly find these Monophysite formulations mythological.

Since we certainly cannot further explain the 'how' of the hypostatic union (and don't in fact have to), these official church formulas ultimately say no more to us than that God in himself has communicated himself to us as our absolute future, reconciliation and forgiveness, and that he has done so in the one whole reality and history of Jesus, from the beginning to the end of his own eternal definitiveness. If we understand and believe that, then we are Christians.

But the traditional doctrinal formulations of the Church on Christology do prevent us from reducing Jesus to the level of a religious genius; of a religious prophet (even one still without an equal), after whom fundamentally new and similar types can come. Perhaps we are slow today to offer structures of thought and terms and concepts which would perhaps enable us in the future to express and preserve the mystery of Jesus in other than the traditional terms, in formulas more directly accessible to us today. Perhaps we need formulas which help us more to avoid the danger of a Monophysite identification of God and man in Jesus, without that leading to another heresy — a new version of an old Nestorianism (as it was understood by the Church in the fifth century), which sees Jesus, ultimately, as no more than an ordinary even if divinely gifted man. But even if other kinds of Christological expression become conceivable in the future, and are composed and perhaps even accepted by the official teaching Church, now as in the future the traditional Christological formulations retain their significance.

A believing and pious Christian can (and indeed must) now say: At Christmas God's Word became flesh and dwelled among us. He says so because that statement is true, asserts what is decisively Christian, and must not be misunderstood. Today too we must proclaim the Christmas message that God became man.

The mystery of the Trinity

Christmas depends on the mystery of the Trinity. The dogma that the one God subsists in three Persons can cause us in our present climate of thought to slip into serious misunderstandings and heresy. The Church, of course, does not teach that there are three 'freedoms' in God, three different centres of consciousness and action which are distinct from one another. That would be tantamount to the heresy of Tritheism, at the most thinly veiled beneath the purely verbal statement that these persons, understood thus, were nevertheless 'one' God.

But if we say that in salvation history, in its culmination in Jesus, God reveals himself as the uncreate
and Inconceivable and therefore is called the Father;
that he reveals himself as the one who in spite of his
continuing inconceivability and uncreated nature can
express himself really as himself in history in his 'Son'
Jesus; that he reveals himself as the one who can est-
ablish himself as himself, as the Spirit, in the innermost
centre of our existence, without surrendering his own
Godhead or dissolving the finite creature in this self-
communication, then we have (only indicated) what
we call the Trinity of salvation history: the threefold
reality of the God who gives himself to us as our eternal
salvation.

When we see that in these three aspects of God's
self-communication to us, it is really a question of
God himself, as he is in himself; that these three 'modalities' of God's self-communication are not simply
mere modes of our reception of this self-communi-
cating God (because they would then be creaturely,
and would involve a self-communication of God by
means of finite characteristics on our side), then we
should have to say that these three modalities of God's
action in salvation-history inhere in him and belong to
him as he is from eternity and for himself. We would
say that this Trinity of the economy of salvation is
necessarily also an immanent Trinity; that God (if we
wish to say so, in order to avoid the word 'person',
which is ambiguous these days) exists in three modes of
subsistence, which at one and the same time comprise
the particularity of his own eternal life *and* the possibility of that communication to us in which he gives
himself to us.

The Trinity of God's self-communication

We can understand that immanent Trinity of God best if we try to think of it from the viewpoint of his self-communication to us; on the sole presupposition that (not to obscure the absolute nature of this self-communication) we understand the Trinity of self-communication as the Trinity of God in himself. Then we can say: the eternal inconceivable uncreate God, called the 'Father', expresses himself historically and subsists in this possibility from eternity as Logos, as Word. From eternity he has the possibility of giving himself as the Spirit of love and entering thus into the innermost centre of created existence. In that possibility, in which he subsists from eternity, he is called Spirit.

Using an authentic 'descent Christology', we can say that the Word that pre-existed from God in eternity became flesh; that the eternal Word of God descended into our history. We can call that Word the eternal Son of the Father, even though we must not deny that the biblical Word of the Son of the Father (at least in the oldest layers of the New Testament) refers primarily to the Man Jesus, insofar as he enjoys that unique union with God (as Word) which distinguishes him from all other men, and through which he is the insurpassable self-donation of God to us.

The Trinitarian theology which is already given in the New Testament and was conceptually systematized in later Christian history may be rather tiresome today. It certainly doesn't have to be placed at the starting-point of the unfolding of our own faith. But without reducing our consciousness of faith in an unhistorical way, we cannot suddenly free ourselves from that common faith history.

The Trinitarian theology which was summarily formulated by the Council of Florence in the fifteenth century does not have to be read as a profession and direct expression of an existentially complete faith. But for us it is an assurance that God-in-himself gives himself to us with his own glory: that he himself, and not a created gift representing him in unavoidably permanent provisionality, is the centre of our existence and our absolute future; and that he has irrevocably and historically communicated himself, as that precisely, in Jesus of Nazareth.

At Christmas, therefore, we should not proclaim the mystery of this feast and receive it into our hearts as if the mystery of the one, triune God were not also part of Christian faith. Of course we should not allow our religious life to get hung up on subtle theological formulations. We must see the credal formulas as guides for faith and life today. We must be able to say now: The eternal Word of the Father has appeared in human flesh, has taken on our reality and history as his own; and has communicated himself to us victoriously and irrevocably.

We have reached the end of what is now a very theoretical and abstract meditation. We must return to the beginning. At Christmas (and, if we are sober and honest, only thus can we truly rejoice), we must avoid a spurious 'Christmas spirit' of unknown provenance and with no real connexion with the Christian mystery of Christmas.

8 Lighten our darkness

It isn't really enjoyable to comment on the Lord's birth at this time. Those who hear or read won't really change.

Every year it's the same. A little uplift. A few pious and humanitarian phrases. A few gifts with the subsequent annoyance of having to say Thank you, even though one would rather have had nothing. And then everything goes on as before.

If one is a Christian one ought not to join in the nonsensical aspect of Christmas. A Christian of all men shouldn't hide the miserable reality of life with pious words. As a sign of his faith, a Christian hangs up a cross: a gallows with a man nailed on it. He hangs it on the walls that hem him in and restrict his life. For him Christmas can be only the beginning of a life which in this world ends on the cross (or in death, or in the empty misery of total disillusionment: it all comes to the same thing — in the end).

After Christmas everything goes on as before. We

shall get along. A long way. To Mars or further still. To an oil crisis and inflation. Finally we shall get to death. But death is something that decent people, East or West, prefer not to talk about. That wouldn't do. It wouldn't do at all. The most you hear about death is some kind of pseudo-philosophical or existentialist rubbish — an intellectual's uplift, written to make a bit on the side.

What should we do then? Creep around in intense piety? Or carry on with 'Christmas', because it's bad form to show how one feels? We could consider what Christmas really means, in a Christian sense. That could be of interest to non-Christians too. We could ask whether in spite of all the banality and ugliness of life, there is not inside a person, deep down inside him (whether he is officially Christian or not) the improbable courage needed to believe in Christmas: in the true Christmas, whether one acknowledges it, or only thinks of it as something that just can't be believed. The courage to believe in this way, which exists within in genuine, tranquil common sense and collectedness of mind, and which enables us to cope with life, presupposes that such common sense is more than the visible aspect of ultimate despair at the meaninglessness of our existence.

The mystery

Because God made Christmas without asking us, it is possible that we believe more than we admit; more, that is, than we acknowledge in our theories about ourselves and our life. How is that?

We always look beyond ourselves. That is no small burden. We are liberated and responsible for ourselves; we are hopers. We extend beyond the given and obvious, the set and determined. We live the conceivable by virtue of the inconceivable. We discover our foundations in the unfathomable depths of the nameless and unutterable. Of course we can pretend that we are anaesthetized to that aspect of things. We can say that it means nothing to us. We can try to hold onto the everyday and perceptible face of things, refusing to turn towards that inconceivable light which first enables us to see all that we think is actually in the light. But mystery permeates all existence. It constantly forces us to look at it, even when it is silent; even when it dazzles us in the joy that knows no object any longer and in the fear that dissolves the self-obviousness of our existence; in the love which acknowledges itself as unconditional and everlasting; in the responsibility which recognizes no earthly court of judgment; and in the question which is terrified at its unconditional nature and unlimited extent.

In the midst of the commonsense everyday movement of life, we are constantly faced with the mystery which is infinite: that mystery which grounds and establishes without itself having any ground; the mystery which is always there and is beyond injury. Nameless, always, everywhere, it prevails in our life. It is not the trace of something that is not as yet enlightened; it is that which is never diminished by any increase in knowledge. If we do not forget thought for the sake of what we think, joy for the sake of giving joy, responsibility for the sake of that to which we have responded, the everlasting future for the sake of the present moment, and unending hope for what we have fought for in the here and now, then we are concerned with God; whether we give that or some other name to the namelessness which we then encounter. An atheist is a man who stubbornly refuses freely to turn from this or that everyday ordinary awareness to the One, the All-encompassing, the All-supporting, who, in knowledge and freedom, is always at the basis of his everyday concerns.

Trusting in mystery

If we accept this thinking, loving, hoping existence in spite of all the hasty, impatient pains and protests on the surface of our life; if we do not confuse responsibility with banality; then we have already given ourselves to God, and opened ourselves to him. Many people do that, even when they think they do not know God (we always have to know him as the Inconceivable, otherwise we have confused him with something else, which is an error that the self-confessed believers fall into all too often), even when in silent respect they do not trust themselves to speak his name.

In that kind of accepted existence, which obediently entrusts itself to mystery, as that to which we are subject and not that to which we are subject, something happens that we call 'grace' in our Christian terminology. God is and remains mystery. But he is the profundity in which human existence is accepted. He is the nearness and not merely the instance. He is forgiveness and not merely judgment. He silently and unutterably answers and fulfils the eternal human question, the groundlessness of hope and the infinite requirements of love. And he does all that of himself.

He does so silently and in that ground of our being which only opens itself to us if we obediently allow ourselves to be encompassed by that mystery, without ever wishing to conquer and rule it. If that happens, then Christmas has already come in us: that arrival of God which Christians acknowledge as occurring out of God's free grace in every man and in the ordinary everyday life of every man who does not reject it out of guilt; out of that guilt which unites fear of God and proud self-sufficiency.

But we are men in history; we are men of the conceivable, perceptible, here-and-now world. God's arrival has to be conceivable and irrevocable as his action upon us, as his deed done to us; it has to be irrevocably and historically conceivable both as the self-giving of God and as the coming of God in a man finally accepted by men. Therefore men have made the experience of this coming something ultimately insurpassable and irrevocable in their history too. They have done so in Jesus of Nazareth.

In Jesus, surrender to everlasting mystery is there as a human act, which is itself grace — like everything that is freedom and decision. In Jesus God, as the unutterable mystery (which he remains), has expressed himself wholly and irrevocably as the word. In Jesus the word is there, as something addressed to us all, as the God of closeness, of unutterable intimacy and forgiveness. In Jesus there is question. In Jesus there is answer. Unmixed and yet inseparable, question and answer have become one. The One is there in whom God and man are one, without any reciprocal cancellation. His self-surrender to mystery is borne by mystery itself. It is not only an action of theory and emotion, but the act of life as a whole in all its dimensions. Therefore it finds its absolute culmination in his death, in which he voluntarily allows himself to fall as it were into the final coming of the mystery before which man is trustingly silent. For Jesus as for us, therefore, Christmas is the beginning of death. Because that death permeates the entire length and breadth of our life and is not merely something at its end that doesn't as yet concern us; because in our everyday life we are always trying to accept that day already; if we live soberly though not banally, we are able to celebrate Christmas with due sobriety.

Celebrating Christmas with sobriety and good cheer

If some have the courage to believe expressly in the truth of Christmas, whereas others silently accept the insurpassable depth of their existence, which is filled with blessed hope, they can all celebrate Christmas together. Then, in the end, there is a certain truth and profundity even in the apparently superficial and conventional bourgeois Christmas. That does not mean that the outward element of chicanery in all the bustle and fuss is the ultimate truth. Behind it all there is the holy and silent truth: the truth that God has indeed come, and that he celebrates Christmas with us.

We enter even more honestly and profoundly into the truth of our lives, if we pass beyond an initial (and only too justifiable) scepticism about the bourgeois Christmas; if we go beyond it soberly yet not taking our own scepticism too seriously; if we celebrate it as the sign that God's future among us far exceeds and excels all our plans and all our disappointments and the banality of life in which we threaten to stay enmeshed. We celebrate it too as the sign that God's truth in Jesus' birth has finally testified that that is so. If after Christmas everything goes on as it was before, it is still true that God has accepted us. In the midst of our genuinely and soberly lived everyday life, the depths of our existence are revealed as a profundity that bourgeois soberness cannot cover in trivial fuss and concerns. Those depths are filled with the grace of the inconceivable mystery that we call God. We can indeed celebrate Christmas with due sobriety and yet good cheer.

Birth in the night

We do not know — historically, that is —whether Jesus

was really born at night. The shepherds' report, the account given by those who were keeping watch over their flocks and heard the heavenly proclamation of the birth of the Saviour, is not in itself unambiguous evidence of a birth in the night. Yet Christians have always portrayed this holy and saving birth as happening at night.

Night has a double aspect. Like almost all the powers of human existence it has two meanings. Night can be the sinister darkness, the time in which no one can do anything. As Jesus says in the Bible, it seems to be related to death. It is the time of the unnatured; of uncertainty and danger; of the unseen. In religion nighttime can have a symbolic meaning too. In Scripture 'night' is the time of unbelief and sin; the time of judgment and divine visitation. Therefore Christians must be children of the daytime. They must shine like stars in the night, so that they are not surprised by the judge who comes like a thief in the night. We have to stay awake; we dare not sleep; instead we must rise up from our beds and walk about as if it were day.

But men see night in another way, as Scripture acknowledges. Night is also the time of stillness and silence and recollected energy; the time which can wait and in which things mature. In the middle of the night we hear the news that the Bridegroom is coming. In the Bible night is the time of heavenly dreams. Because night is the time of release from the enslaving impressions and bonds of external everyday life, it is a time of prayer. Jesus spent entire nights in dialogue with his Father. Night can also be experienced poignantly as God's creation. The psalmist prays (Ps 74. 16): Thine is day, thine also the night. Daniel (3. 71) asks the night to praise God just as, according to the psalmist, every night announces to the next the news of the majesty of God. In Psalm 19, night to night declares the knowledge of the Lord to the hearts of the pious.

How do we experience the night in these two ways? We know it as beginning, as that which is yet undetermined, indefinite, to which the precision of day and its light has yet to come. But the beginning and possibility are ambiguous: the good promise that is as yet unfilled, the broad free possibility which however has not yet found its due reality; the marvellous plan which still hasn't been carried out. That is necessarily ambiguous: promise, yet a promise under threat; a forerunner with access to the most distant future, but to one we are not certain will come.

If there is a moment in history (individual history and that of humanity as a whole) which is like a first beginning, full of insurpassable possibilities and promises, a beginning which holds everything in its mysterious womb; and if this onset of unutterable, infinite beginning most assuredly already bears its realization within it, is already certain of its victory, and is just as much fulfilment as it is promise, then that moment deserves to be called the Holy Night. 'Night', because it is beginning; 'holy' because it is blessed and invincible beginning. We have to call such a beginning the holy night, the blessed night, the sacred night. And so we do when we sing: Silent night, holy night. That greeting to the feast of the Lord's coming is sung throughout the world. During the fourth century the feast of Christmas was quite deliberately established at the time when for nature the sun seems to begin its course anew. They set the beginning of the 'sun of righteousness' (as the prophet calls the Saviour) on the day of the pagan *natalis solis invicti*, on the feast-day of the 'invincible sun-god'.

They were right to do that. For Christian belief says that was when it began. That was when God calmly slipped out of the terrible blaze in which he dwelled as God and Lord, and came to us. He entered silently into the hut of our earthly existence, as a man. He began where we begin: quite poor, quite defenceless; as a child, gentle and unarmed. He who is the everlasting distant future which we from our position in time can never encompass, because it seems to stretch into ever greater distances ahead as we hurry towards it on the hard roads of our existence, he himself came among us. Since otherwise we should not find him, together with us he took our way to him. He did so to find a proper ending, for that end in Jesus also became our beginning.

God is close to us. His eternal word of mercy and loving-kindness occurs where we now are. He is a pilgrim on our paths. He shares our joys and our suffering. He lives our life and dies our death. Softly, tenderly, he has put his eternal life into this world and into its death.

He has redeemed us, for he has shared our lot. He has made our beginning his own beginning. He has passed along our path of fate and thereby opened it into the unending spaces of God. Since the Word of God has accepted us irrevocably, since he never ceases to be man, our and his beginning is an onset of indestructible promises, and this beginning, quiet as night, is our Holy Night.

Celebrating Christmas

That is some indication of how we should celebrate Christmas: as the mystery of the Holy Night. Christmas must be quiet and peaceful, collected and gentle in our hearts. It must be without any reservations, like a child's heart that as yet sees none of the possibilities of his existence, but is guilelessly ready for all of them. The profundity, breadth and inconceivability of our being must quietly prevail, like the night, by banishing the obviously graspable and measured things. It has to bring the distant future close without diminishing it. We must allow this quiet of the night to enter into the inward man, by avoiding flight into the concern, sweat, noise and fuss in which we try to get away from ourselves and the mystery above us, for the great mystery of infinite love astonishes and frightens us who are so unused to it.

We should not degrade with cheap celebrations this Holy Night in which our life too was dedicated. The childlike aspect of this feast, however, which suits such a day, should remain open to that unutterable mystery which first makes men profoundly aware of one another, and offers them the promise of eternal youth. The man who in the peace of gentle reserve, of submissiveness, in the silent holy nighttime of his own heart, lets the multitude and tumult of things, people and worries recede, which would otherwise obscure his vision of infinity; the man who even only for a short time extinguishes earthly lights which otherwise would obscure the lights of heaven; the man who in that silent night of the heart allows himself to be summoned by the unutterable, unspeaking closeness of God, whose voice is its silence, if we have ears to hear it; only that man celebrates Christmas as it should be celebrated if it is not to be debased to the level of a purely secular feast-day. Our Christmas must be as if we were walking on a clear winter's night beneath a starry sky. Far off there is still the light and welcome shelter of human habitation, but above us is the sky. The silent night which would otherwise seem sinister and threatening becomes the quiet closeness of the infinite mystery of our existence, which is both sheltering love and inconceivable grandeur.

God is close to us

It will soon be the holy night of the Lord's coming, The eternal future has come into our time. Its light still dazzles us, so much so that we think it is night. But it is a blessed night; a night which is already full of warmth and light; full of beauty, and mysterious and protective because of the eternal day which it carries in its dark womb. It is a silent and holy night. But is is so only if we let the holy silence of this night into our inwardness, if our hearts too keep lonely watch by night. They can easily do so. For that solitariness and quiet are easy. Their difficulty is only that proper to all elevated things which are simple and yet great. We *are* lonely. There is an inner country in our hearts where we are alone, where no one but God can dwell. The question is only whether we do not avoid it in fear born of foolish guilt, because no one and no part of all that we trust in on earth can go there with us. We must enter softly, and close the door behind us. There we must listen to the unique music played in the silence of that night where the quiet and solitary soul sings to the God of its heart. There it sings its softest and most inward music. It knows that God is listening as it sings. The music of the soul no longer has to reach the God of its love beyond the stars where he dwells in inaccessible light beyond human perception.

Because it is our Holy Night, because the Word became flesh, God is close to us, and the word of love, the softest word in the noiseless space of the human heart, reaches the ear and heart of God.

PART THREE

9 Faith, hope and love

Faith

Faith looks up at the Lord's cross. The first thing the cross has to say to the believer about his life is a fact: a simple but awful fact, for it determines life as a whole: the fact that the cross, whatever name it may be given, is among the things in a man's life he can never really escape from.

The cross came to have a terrible and unique importance in Jesus' life. But everywhere new events occur, again and again, before whose darkness and sheer horror we just stand dumb and helpless as we do before the execution of Jesus. In the end, human history numbers not the fortunate *and* the unfortunate, the victors *and* the vanquished, but − if we see a whole lifetime in relation to its ending − only the vanquished. There are only men who in a thousand ways − poverty, illness, failure, narrow circumstances, vile social injustice, guilt and, ultimately, death − are cast into that deadly silent inconceivability which radiates loneliness and which Christians call − perhaps too conventionally and pietistically − 'the cross'.

We can't get rid of the cross. It marks our life until it

conquers in death and is erected on our grave as a sign of our subjection. Of course we can and must guard against all evil in society and in our private life. And the message of the cross must not be misunderstood: it does not stand for inactivity and as consolation for people for whom we should be fighting hard. But that doesn't alter the fact that we are all on our way towards death, and that death is indwelling in life. It doesn't alter the fact that our life is a way of the cross into death; into its loneliness and inconceivability.

When our faith looks on Jesus' cross, it is asked a question: whether it can stand up to the knowledge that the cross is inevitable. Clear-headed realism about the nature of life is of course the first thing demanded of a Christian when he is asked to take up his cross and follow Jesus. But there is a strong temptation for the individual and society to hide their own situation, to veil its harsh reality, and to suppress the word the cross speaks to us.

We have to struggle against the cross. In life and in society we continually win partial and often quite impressive victories over death. That should make us rejoice. Whenever possible, we should rejoice at the power of life, of mind and body. We should always live in hope of further partial conquests. But we must never forget the fact of the cross. All joy in life must live in tacit acknowledgment of the word spoken by the cross.

That brings us to a question every man has to ask himself quietly but resolutely: Where is the cross in my life that I don't want to see, that I wouldn't willingly take up? The one that becomes the blessed cross of Christ when we do look at it unflinchingly and willingly take it up? That question is addressed to every man, and every man has to give his own answer to it. If a mature person says that it has never come up in his life, he is either someone whom — perhaps quite secretly — the power of Jesus' cross has already beaten down, or someone who in terrible blindness has not yet reached his life's main question. But the question *is* asked of us all, and everyone has to answer it in his own way.

Hope

Hope looks up at Jesus' cross. The hope I am talking of here is the one hope which bears and encompasses everything, whose meaning and power is God, and which knows as it contemplates the cross of Jesus that it is called and justified. The opposite is absolute despair, which can also exist very quietly, deep down in a person's life, and is possible as a man's own freely-chosen guilt. But if a man is so torn by anguish, suffering and death that he loses his own free self-possession and any real self-control and responsibility, a kind of despair can also be present which has no trace of guilt and despair in a personal sense. Then a man is not an agent of his despair but a purely passive creature from whom God has taken responsibility, in order to take it upon himself and his inconceivable mercy and loving-kindness (even though, in our limited view, the fate of that man or woman in so desperate a state seems as ghastly as anything possibly could be).

There are many hopes in our life which wither and fade away. But do we hope that unique hope given by God himself, the hope which supports and encompasses everything, which does not vanish but remains in all the vicissitudes of our other hopes? We have many hopes. We hope for health, victory over disease, success in life, love and security, peace in the world, and a thousand other things which our life's deep force stretches out towards. All these hoped-for things are good in themselves. For a time and in part we experience the fulfilment of those hopes. But in the end they are all deceived. They fade or capsize, whether they were fulfilled at one time, or remain unfulfilled. For we are on our way towards death. On our way there, one after the other, our hopes are taken from us. What then?

What now, indeed? Now, when in a quiet moment, or in the midst of life's noise, we are overcome by the ultimate hopelessness of our hoping? What if the lights of life which illuminate our everyday existence went out one after the other? If evening and night cast everything into a primal unspeaking irreality? When all hopes are dead, is despair the only thing remaining? Or is that dead moment perhaps the moment of the one, unique all-embracing hope? A Christian bears witness to the experience that, in the very death of hopes, hope itself can rise us and conquer. There is nothing individual and specific to hold onto. But the one Inconceivability which encompasses all things (and whose true name is God) quietly supports man and raises him up. If you allow yourself to be borne up, trusting that this Inconceivability is the true and blessed home of man, then you learn that you need no longer hold on in order to be held; that you need no longer fight in order to win; that you need no longer rush after this or that, hoping that it might be so, in order to hope in the one inconceivable Hope which is present to itself and yet bears unutterable fulfilment within itself.

There is something else in Christian hope: knowledge that Jesus in the very movement of defeat is victorious. These two aspects (letting oneself fall into the inconceivability of God, into unutterable blessedness, *and* recognition of the victory of Jesus in his mortal defeat) determine and support one another in a Christian. Together they make up the one Christian hope. When, in the experience of his own banality and guilt, a man is in danger of despairing of himself, he nevertheless knows when he looks at Jesus the selfless and holy Lord, that he may not allow, this time at least, his life to drop despairing into empty meaninglessness. He realizes that he must confess Jesus as the one who lives with God for ever. He realizes therefore that he should hope the one true hope; for this crucified Man loved him too, right up to the end. At such moments, the experience of God as the one hope in the failure of all our hopes combines with faith in the Crucified to produce the one Christian hope. Do we hope that hope? The one and only hope? Can we pray with the Church: Hail O Cross our only hope?

Love

Finally love has to study the love of the Crucified for us: to contemplate that reciprocal love between Jesus and a Christian. Essentially, this love can be understood only by the lover in loving. All reflection on it is ultimately inadequate because what is primarily in question is the love of God's crucified Son and the love which redeems our whole existence. Nevertheless, we can ask humbly: Did the Crucified Jesus love us and therefore me, on the cross? Can I really love him?

Did Jesus love me on the cross? Could he possibly know about me as I actually am, as my unique self? Could he know about me in the Godforsaken darkness and terrible impotence of his death? Was there room for me in this dying Jesus? Does that love reach me over all that space and time? Does it reach out to me where I have to live and die, here and now? Our answer must be a faithful Yes, even if we do not know how such love is possible in the heart of a finite man and in the darkness of death. Scripture testifies to it from its living experience of the Spirit of Jesus. He loved me and gave himself for me. Learned theologians have tried to explain the possibility of this love, which is testified to in the Bible. They have interpreted it as a sign of the absolute unity of the divine Word and the human reality of Jesus, the union of the divine and the human consciousness, a union that makes it possible for Jesus' human consciousness to know every single man and woman.

Try to look at it another way. The dimensions and levels of human relationships, the very dimensions which make love possible, are different. That means that there are very different modes of love: superficial love, everyday love, and the absolute love at the very core of existence. The fact that we are physically close to one another and that we feel friendly towards one another does not imply absolute love, which remains an ultimately profound thing. But when someone, in blessed light or mortal darkness, really let himself drop and unconditionally surrenders himself to that unfathomable mystery (which tears him from himself, thus making possible the ultimate love which is surrender , and is at the same time the origin and goal of all realities and all men), then that One who sacrifices himself out of love in all death's darkness has in fact reached the innermost ground of all reality and is close to all men. Jesus loves us all. He loves me because he has quite ignored himself. Therefore he has reached out in death from the inconceivable midpoint of all reality (which we call God) to everything and therefore to me as well, and he has reached me for ever.

Can I love Jesus? Is that kind of love only an odd, unreal mental affair? Is it introverted piety: a substitute for real love which we should feel for an actual human being who meets us really and physically in everyday life? We can answer that question only from the twenty-fifth chapter of Matthew and the first letter of John. According to Scripture, you can love God and Jesus truly only by loving your actual neighbour. If you love your neighbour without reservation and venture your whole existence in that love, then such love is already (expressly or unconsciously) a breakthrough to that reality in which God and man are irrevocably united, in which God guarantees the possibility and the blessed outcome of the venture of human love, and will not allow it to fail in the end, but in that union makes it possible for man to love God himself humanly and in a human being.

But that union is the God-man Jesus Christ. The love for one's neighbour which cannot of itself defend itself against the suspicion that it is an absurd bet, is therefore, when it nevertheless becomes an absolute venture, a breakthrough to love of the God-man, whether one is consciously aware of it or not. But the Christian is aware of it. If he really tries to love his neighbour, he is entitled to hope that in that love he also loves Jesus, and in prayer and hope can expressly make that love the centre of his life.

Love looks at the crucified Jesus, and the Christian knows: I am encompassed by an everlasting love, even in all the emptiness of my disappointments, my suffering, my death-sentence and my guilt. A Christian knows: This love all about me sets me free to love God and man.